One Pot Chef
Dinner Winner

by David Chilcott

One Pot Chef Dinner Winner

ISBN: 978-1-105-88926-4

Written by David Chilcott

Cover Design by ChoppA

http://www.youtube.com/CakesByChoppA

Postal Address:

One Pot Chef Show

PO Box 4338

Bay Village NSW 2261

Australia

Official Website:

http://www.onepotchefshow.com

Watch My Cooking Videos:

http://www.youtube.com/onepotchefshow

For Dad

*Thanks for all the love and support through the years. Your wisdom and wit have shaped the man I am.
I am blessed to have such an awesome father.*

Table Of Contents

Introduction

Dinner is usually the major meal of the day. But it seems to carry a much larger social significance. Dinner brings the family together at the end of a long day. We discuss the day's events over a hot meal, trade stories and bond with our kin.

Dinner can be used as a way of solidifying new relationships. How many times have we invited new friends over to share a meal? It's no coincidence that most romantic relationships start with a dinner date. Even people in business conduct meetings and combine work with fine dining. Clearly, it's a major part of our lives.

So it's sad that the art of creating a nice, home cooked meal seems to be on the decline. Many children now grow up in homes where neither parent cooks on a regular basis. Aside from the health issues that arise with a diet of fast food, frozen microwave meals and the like, frequently families that don't cook on a regular basis miss out of that crucial bonding experience that comes with making and sharing a meal together.

So this book is written with the hope that it will help to inspire a change. I hope that with these simple recipes, we can help to bring back the idea of family togetherness. A family that cooks together, stays together!

But beyond the social benefits, cooking is an essential life skill. It helps to develop a sense of independence and achievement. Eating a well prepared meal that you made yourself is a very satisfying experience. A kitchen that is rarely used is a sad and lonely thing, and I've always felt a home is never complete without the smells and sounds of an active kitchen.

Within these pages, you'll find an array of fun, easy to prepare meals that anyone can cook. No complicated equipment. No hard-to-find ingredients. Just delicious food that you and your family will adore. Adapt them to suit your own personal tastes, and hopefully you may find some new "family favorites" to add to your collection.

I hope you enjoy this book.

David Chilcott

The One Pot Chef

Perfect Pasta

Delicious Meals in Minutes

I don't know where I would be without pasta. It's a glorious invention that has made the preparation of main meals a million times easier. My kitchen cupboards are never without a selection of pastas in various shapes, sizes and colours.

My Mother always said "If you have a bag of pasta in the pantry, you're halfway to a great meal" and she couldn't be more correct. It's so convenient to be able to throw some pasta into a pot of boiling water and in about 10 minutes, you have a simple but filling meal base that goes with an endless array of recipes.

These days, with busy schedules and diminishing free time, it's comforting to know that a slap-up pasta dinner is only moments away. Now of course, you are welcome to buy one of those fancy, complicated pasta making machines – complete with fidgety add-ons and cleaning instructions that will make you want to tear your hair out. But the majority of people are happy with dry pasta. It's cheap, it keeps well in the pantry and it's quick to cook.

Above all else, pasta is very filling. You don't need to eat a huge amount of it to get a full, satisfying meal. A little pasta, a nice sauce, maybe a little side salad and you'll feel like you've eaten an 12-course meal. Which makes it perfect for those living on a tight food budget. Pasta can help stretch a meal out and make it last longer, or feed more people.

Now before I get beaten to death by those carb-counting fitness weirdos – I'm certainly not advocating a diet of nothing but pasta. Obviously, a varied and balanced diet is best. But adding pasta dishes to your regular meal rotation is a great time-saving and indeed money-saving option that is well worth exploring.

I have no idea whether pasta was originally invented by the Italians or the Chinese. To be honest, I think there will be arguments about that for many years to come. But to whoever was responsible for this remarkable foodstuff – I most graciously thank you for the many delicious meals I have enjoyed because of your genius. I salute you!

Pasta Carbonara

Ingredients	Method
250g of Pasta (cooked as per packet directions) **250ml of Cream** **2 Egg Yolks** **1/2 Cup of Freshly Grated Parmesan Cheese (plus extra for garnish)** **3 Slices of Shortcut Rindless Bacon (chopped)** **Freshly Cracked Black Pepper**	1) In a small mixing bowl, add egg yolks, cream and cheese. Season with pepper. Whisk mixture to combined. 2) Fry bacon in a fry pan until cooked. Transfer to a plate and set aside. 3) Cook pasta as per packet directions until tender. Drain and return to the pot. Stir through bacon. 4) Over a medium heat and working quickly, stir through the cream mixture ensuring all the pasta is nicely coated. Stir for 2-3 minutes or until sauce is slightly thickened. Divide between serving bowls or plates and garnish with extra cheese. Serve immediately.

Preparation Time: 5 Minutes

Cooking Time: 10 Minutes

Serves 2

Pasta Boscaiola

Ingredients	Method
500g Pasta (cooked following packet instructions)	1) Cook pasta in a large saucepan, following packet directions, until tender. Drain and set aside.
500ml of Cream (I used Heavy Cream)	
150g of Bacon (about 3 large slices, chopped)	2) In a small mixing bowl, add cream and stock. Season with salt and pepper, then stir until combined. Set aside.
1 Brown Onion (chopped)	
2 Cloves of Garlic (crushed)	3) In a small pan over medium heat, add a splash of oil and fry onions, garlic and bacon for about 6 minutes. Add mushrooms and stir. Cook, covered, for a further 3 minutes, stir occasionally, until mushrooms are tender.
200g of Button Mushrooms (sliced)	
1/2 Cup of Chicken Stock	
Fresh Parsley (chopped)	4) Add cream mixture to large pot. Heat over a medium heat until almost boiling. Add cooked pasta and bacon mixture. Stir through parsley. Stir over low heat until everything is warmed through. Serve.
Olive Oil	
Salt and Pepper	

Preparation Time: 10 Minutes

Cooking Time: 20 Minutes

Serves 4

Spaghetti Puttanesca

Ingredients	Method
2 Tablespoons of Olive Oil **2 Cloves of Crushed Garlic (About 2 Teaspoons)** **1 Small Red Chilli (deseeded and chopped)** **6 Anchovy Fillets (chopped)** **1 Tablespoon of Tomato Paste** **2 Tablespoons of Fresh Basil (chopped)** **100g of Pitted Black Olives (sliced)** **800g Can of Diced Tomatoes** **Salt and Pepper** **500g Spaghetti (cooked)**	1) Cook pasta in a large saucepan, following packet directions, until tender. Drain and return to saucepan. Set aside. 2) In another saucepan, add oil, garlic, chilli and anchovies. Cook over a low heat, stirring, for about 2 minutes. 3) Add tomato paste, basil, olives and tomatoes. Season with salt and pepper then increase temperature to medium and allow sauce to come to the boil. 4) Reduce temperature and allow to simmer for 15 minutes or until slightly thickened. 5) Pour sauce over cooked pasta and toss to coat. Serve immediately.

Preparation Time: 5 Minutes

Cooking Time: 15 Minutes

Serves 4

Tuna Macaroni Bake

Ingredients	Method
500g Macaroni (cooked following packet directions)	1) Cook pasta in a large saucepan, following packet directions, until tender. Drain and return to saucepan. Set aside.
400g Can of Tuna (drained and flaked with a fork)	
2 Cups of Frozen Mixed Vegetables	2) In another saucepan, add butter and melt over a medium heat. Add flour and stir. Cook for 1 minute or until bubbling. Gradually pour in milk while whisking mixture. Continue to whisk for about 3 minutes or until sauce thickens. Remove from heat. Stir in 1 cup of cheese until melted. Season with salt and pepper.
2 Cups of Grated Cheese	
3 Cups of Milk	
1/4 Cup of Plain Flour	
50g Butter	
1 Cup of Fresh Breadcrumbs (about 2 slices of bread)	3) Add vegetables, tuna and cheese sauce to pasta. Stir until thoroughly mixed. Spoon mixture into a large baking dish. Sprinkle with breadcrumbs and remaining cheese. Bake in a preheated oven for 20 minutes at 180 degrees Celsius, or until top is golden and cheese is melted. Serve immediately.

Preparation Time: 10 Minutes

Cooking Time: 20 Minutes

Serves 6 – 8

Macaroni and Cheese

Ingredients	Method
500g Pack of Macaroni (or other pasta) **1 Litre of Milk (4 Cups)** **60g Butter** **1/3 Cup of Plain Flour** **1 Cup of Grated Cheddar Cheese** **1/2 Cup of Freshly Grated Parmesan Cheese (plus extra for topping)** **Salt and Pepper (to season)**	1) Cook pasta in a large saucepan, following packet directions, until tender. Drain and return to saucepan. Set aside. 2) In another saucepan, add butter and melt over a medium heat. Add flour and stir. Cook for 1 minute or until bubbling. Gradually pour in milk while whisking mixture. Continue to whisk until sauce thickens. Remove from heat. Stir in 1 cup of cheese until melted. Season with salt and pepper. 3) Top with extra cheese and bake in a preheated oven for 20 minutes at 180 degrees Celsius, or until top is golden and cheese is melted. Serve immediately.

Preparation Time: 10 Minutes

Cooking Time: 20 Minutes

Serves 6 – 8

Quick Cheesy Pasta Bake

Ingredients	Method
500g Pasta (Macaroni, Penne or Spirals work well) 1 Can of Tomato Soup (Add 2 Cans if you want it saucier) 2 Cups of Cooked Chicken Meat 1 Cup of Frozen Mixed Vegetables 2 Cups of Grated Cheese	1) Cook pasta in a large saucepan, following packet directions, until tender. Drain and return to saucepan. 2) Add soup to pasta and stir through. Add chicken, 1 cup of cheese and vegetables. Stir to combine. Transfer to a large baking dish. 3) Top with remaining cheese and bake in a preheated oven for 20 minutes at 180 degrees Celsius, or until top is golden and cheese is melted. Serve immediately.

Preparation Time: 5 Minutes

Cooking Time: 30 Minutes

Serves 6 – 8

Tomato Pesto Pasta Salad

Ingredients	Method
500g Penne Pasta **1 Jar of Tomato Pesto Sauce (about 200g)** **200g of Cooked Chicken Breast Fillet, cubed (I used Poached Chicken)** **Cherry Tomatoes (quartered)** **Freshly Grated Parmesan Cheese** **Freshly Chopped Parsley**	1) Cook pasta in a large saucepan, following packet directions, until tender. Drain and return to saucepan. 2) Stir pesto sauce through pasta, ensuring all pasta is nicely coated. Transfer to a large serving plate. 3) Top pasta with chicken, cherry tomatoes and cheese. Garnish with parsley. Serve warm or chilled.

Preparation Time: 5 Minutes

Cooking Time: 10 Minutes

Serves 6 – 8

Macaroni Salad

Ingredients	Method
500g Macaroni / Small Pasta (cooked according to packet directions) **100g Cheddar Cheese (cubed)** **2 Carrots (grated)** **1 White Onion (chopped)** **2 Celery Sticks (diced)** **2 Large Tomatoes (diced)** **1 Small Can of Pineapple Pieces (drained and chopped)** **1/2 Cup of Sultanas / Raisins** **1 Cup of Mayonnaise** **1-2 Teaspoons of Curry Powder**	1) Cook pasta in a large saucepan, following packet directions, until tender. Drain in a colander and run cold water over pasta until cold. Drain and transfer pasta to a large salad bowl. 2) Make dressing by combining mayonnaise and curry powder in a small jug. Set aside. 3) Add all other ingredients to pasta. Toss to combine. Pour dressing over salad and toss to ensure everything is nicely coated. Serve immediately or chill until required.

Preparation Time: 20 Minutes

Cooking Time: 10 Minutes

Serves 8 - 10

Quick Eats

Fast Meals for Busy Lives

When people think of "fast food" - it usually conjures up images of deep fried nightmares and food that features low quality ingredients. I think that's why I named this section "Quick Eats" as I didn't want to make people think that just because a meal doesn't take long to make, it means it's some horrible mess that you'd get from some cheap fast food chain restaurant.

I'm a busy man. When I'm not filming cooking videos or editing footage, I'm running a full-time business from home. As odd as it might seem, I don't always have time to cook a full main meal with all the bells and whistles every single night. Such a prospect would send me into an hysterical fit and require a trip to a mental hospital.

Sometimes, you just want to get dinner on the table. No mess, no fuss, no endless work in the kitchen or lengthy clean-up sessions. That's what this section is all about. Most of these recipes can be thrown together in about half an hour or so. Some of them only take a few minutes of work, then put it in the oven! You can't complain about that kind of simplicity.

This section is also perfect for people who complain that they simply "don't have time to cook" dinner for themselves. This is a tired excuse that is quickly becoming less and less acceptable. You can't live your life eating nothing but junk food and microwave frozen meals. Aside from being unhealthy – it's just plain boring. Human beings need variety, or they get stuck in routines that quickly turn into ruts.

So not more excuses! Get into the kitchen and make a fabulous dinner in minutes. Start with the Honey Mustard Chicken – it's my personal favourite!

Turkey Burgers

Ingredients	Method
500g Turkey Breast Mince **1/2 Cup of Fresh Bread Crumbs** **1 Egg** **1/2 a Brown Onion (diced)** **1 Clove of Garlic (crushed)** **1/2 Teaspoon of Mild Paprika** **1 Tablespoon of BBQ Sauce** **Fresh Bread Rolls** **Lettuce** **Tomato (sliced)** **Cheese** **Mayonnaise** **Olive Oil** **Salt and Pepper**	1) Preheat oven to 180 degrees Celsius. 2) In a lightly oiled pan, fry the onion and garlic over a medium heat until onions soften. Set aside to cool. 3) In a large mixing bowl, add mince, onion mixture, BBQ sauce, paprika, salt, pepper and breadcrumbs. Use your hands to mix everything together. 4) Divide the mixture to form 6 patties. Place on a plate and chill for 30 minutes or until firm. 5) In a lightly oiled pan, fry patties in batches for about 3-4 minutes each side (or until browned) then transfer to a baking tray lined with non-stick baking paper. 6) Place a slice of cheese on each patty and bake for about 10 minutes or until cooked all the way through and cheese is melted. Serve on bread rolls with lettuce, tomato and mayonnaise.

Preparation Time: 10 Minutes

Cooking Time: 20 Minutes

Serves 6

Beef Chow Mein

Ingredients	Method
500g Beef Mince	1) Heat oil in a wok or large frypan over high heat. Add onion, beef and Chinese Five Spice. Cook stirring for 5 minutes or until meat is browned and broken up.
1 Brown Onion (chopped)	
1 Tablespoon of Vegetable Oil	
2 Teaspoons of Chinese Five Spice	2) Add soy sauce, sweet chilli sauce and water and stir to combine. Bring to the boil.
2 Tablespoons of Soy Sauce	
2 Tablespoons of Sweet Chilli Sauce	3) Add in vegetables and stir for 2 minutes, or until cabbage begins to wilt.
1 Cup of Water	
1/2 a Wombok (Chinese Cabbage)	4) Add noodles and stir to allow noodles to separate. Cook until everything is heated through. Serve immediately.
1 Red Capsicum (Bell Pepper - sliced)	
Handful of Snow Peas	
400g Pack of Thin Egg Noodles	

Preparation Time: 5 Minutes
Cooking Time: 10 Minutes
Serves 6

Chicken Noodle Egg Bake

Ingredients	Method
85g Packet of Two Minute Noodles (aka Ramen) **1/2 Cup of Frozen Peas (or any frozen vegetables)** **Boiling Water** **1 Cup of Shredded Roast Chicken** **3 Eggs** **1 Tablespoon of Worcestershire Sauce** **1 Teaspoon of Minced Garlic (about 1 Clove)** **Salt and Pepper** **1/2 Cup of Grated Cheddar Cheese**	1) Add noodles, peas and contents of noodle flavor packet to a heatproof bowl and cover with boiling water. Stand for 2 minutes or until noodles soften. Drain and transfer to a small baking dish. 2) In a small mixing bowl, add eggs, worcestershire sauce and garlic. Season with salt and pepper, then lightly beat with a fork. 3) Toss chicken through noodles and pour egg mixture over the top. Top with cheese. 4) Bake in a preheated oven at 180 degrees Celsius for about 20 minutes or until golden on top and egg is fully cooked. Serve immediately.

Preparation Time: 5 Minutes

Cooking Time: 20 Minutes

Serves 2 – 4

Toad in the Hole

Ingredients	Method
8 Sausages or Skinless Hot Dogs **2 Tablespoons of Olive Oil** **3/4 Cup of Plain Flour** **1 1/2 Cups of Milk** **2 Eggs** **Salt and Pepper** **1 Teaspoon of Chopped Parsley**	1) Preheat oven to 200 degrees Celsius. 2) In a large mixing jug, add flour, eggs, milk and parsley. Season with salt and pepper. Whisk until smooth. 3) Add oil to a large baking dish, and place in the oven for 5 minutes. Carefully place sausages in the heated dish and return to the oven for 10 minutes, flipping the sausages over (with a pair of tongs) after 5 minutes. 4) Carefully pour the batter over sausages. Return dish to the oven for 30-35 minutes or until batter is puffed up and sausages are fully cooked. 5) Serve with vegetables and gravy.

Preparation Time: 5 Minutes

Cooking Time: About 40 minutes

Serves 4

Honey Mustard Chicken

Ingredients	Method
500g Chicken Thigh Fillets (chopped into small pieces) **2 Tablespoons of Honey** **1 Tablespoon of Dijon Mustard** **1 Tablespoon of Wholegrain Mustard** **2 Tablespoons of White Vinegar** **Oil** **Rice (to serve)** **¼ Cup of Pouring Cream (optional)**	1) In a small jug, add honey, mustards and vinegar. Stir to combine. Place chicken in a mixing bowl and pour mustard mixture over the chicken. Cover with plastic wrap and chill for 30 minutes. 2) In a large fry pan, add a little oil and heat over a medium heat. Add marinated chicken and any residual sauce into the pan. Cook for 5-7 minutes or until chicken is cooked through. Stir through cream (if desired) and cook for a further 2-3 minutes or until completely heated through. 3) Serve with rice.

Preparation Time: 10 Minutes (plus chilling time)

Cooking Time: About 10 minutes

Serves 4

Quick Butter Chicken

Ingredients	Method
1Kg of Chicken Thigh Fillets (chopped) **1 Brown Onion (roughly chopped)** **2 Tablespoons of Butter** **1/4 Cup of Curry Powder (reduce by half for a milder flavor)** **2 x 400g Cans of Tomato Soup** **1/2 Cup of Sour Cream** **Rice (to serve)**	1) Add butter to a large fry pan over medium heat. Once melted, add onions. Cook for 1-2 minutes or until softened. 2) Add chicken and cook stirring for 5 minutes or until almost cooked. Add curry powder and stir. 3) Pour in tomato soup and stir to combine. Bring to the boil then simmer for a further 2-3 minutes or until chicken is fully cooked. Stir in sour cream. Cook for 1 minute or until completely heated through. 4) Serve with rice.

Preparation Time: 10 Minutes

Cooking Time: About 10 minutes

Serves 4

Sausages in Brown Onion Gravy

Ingredients	Method
12 Thin Sausages (I used plain pork sausages) 1 Medium Sized Brown Onion (Peeled and Chopped) 1/2 Cup of Plain Flour Olive Oil 1/4 Cup of Tomato Sauce (Ketchup) 1 Tablespoon of Worcestershire Sauce 2 Cups of Liquid Beef Stock 1 Cup of Water Salt and Pepper	1) In a lightly oiled large fry pan over medium heat, brown the sausages in batches. Slice into chunks and set aside. 2) In a lightly oiled saucepan over medium heat, cook the onion for 2-3 minutes or until softened a lightly browned. Add ketchup, worcestershire sauce and flour. Stir to form a paste. Gradually add in stock and water while whisking. 3) Once gravy is smooth, season with salt and pepper and add the sausages. Stir to combine. Bring to the boil then simmer for 15 minutes or until sausages are cooked through. Serve with potatoes and/or vegetables.

Preparation Time: 5 Minutes

Cooking Time: About 20 minutes

Serves 4-6

Quick Meatball Subs

Ingredients	Method
8 Thin Sausages (or about 500g of Sausage Meat) **4 Sub Style Bread Rolls** **500g Jar of Pasta Sauce** **Olive Oil** **Grated Cheddar Cheese**	1) Snip the ends off each of the sausages using a pair of scissors, then squeeze the meat out into a bowl. Discard the sausage skins. 2) Take spoonfuls of the meat and roll them into balls. Lightly oil a frypan over medium heat and brown the meatballs on all sides. 3) Add the pasta sauce to the meatballs, bring to the boil, then simmer gently until meatballs are cooked through. 4) Spoon meatballs onto bread rolls and top with grated cheese. Serve.

Preparation Time: 5 Minutes

Cooking Time: About 10 minutes

Serves 4

Stuffed Mushrooms

Ingredients	Method
10 Small Cup Mushrooms (stalks removed) **100g Ricotta Cheese** **100g Semi Sun-dried Tomatoes (chopped)** **2 Tablespoons of Fresh Basil (chopped)** **1/4 Cup of Grated Cheddar Cheese** **Salt and Pepper** **Olive Oil**	1) Arrange mushrooms on a baking tray lined with non-stick baking paper. Set aside. 2) In a mixing bowl, add ricotta cheese, tomatoes, grated cheese and basil. Season with salt and pepper. Mix to combine. 3) Spoon mixture into the mushrooms. Use the spoon to form a smooth, rounded dome on top of each mushroom. 4) Bake in a preheated oven at 180 degrees Celsius for 20 minutes. Serve with a side salad or mixed vegetables.

Preparation Time: 10 Minutes
Cooking Time: About 20 minutes
Serves 5

Impossible Quiche

Ingredients	Method
4 Eggs 1 1/2 Cups of Milk 1 1/2 Cups of Grated Cheddar Cheese 150g Shaved Ham (shredded) 1/2 Cup of Self Raising Flour 1 Brown Onion (diced) Salt and Pepper (to season)	1) In a plastic storage container, add onion, ham, cheese and flour. Place the lid on and shake container to coat all ingredients with flour. Set aside. 2) In a large jug, whisk together eggs and milk. Pour into the flour mixture. Stir to combine. 3) Pour mixture into a lightly greased pie plate. Bake in a preheated oven at 200 degrees Celsius or until golden on top and egg mixture is set. 4) Serve warm or cold with side salad or mixed vegetables.

Preparation Time: 5 Minutes

Cooking Time: About 45 minutes

Serves 4-6

Vegetable Pasties

Ingredients	Method
4 Sheets of Ready Rolled Frozen Puff Pastry (partially thawed) **1 Brown Onion (chopped)** **1 Stock Cube (such as Oxo etc)** **2 Medium Sized Potatoes (peeled and diced)** **4 Medium Sized Carrots (peeled and diced)** **1/2 Cup of Frozen Peas**	1) In a lightly greased saucepan over medium heat, add onion and crumbled stock cube. Stir for 2-3 minutes or until onions soften. 2) Add potatoes, carrots and peas. Stir and cook for a further 10 minutes or until vegetables are tender. Remove from heat and set aside to cool. 3) Using a plate as a guide, cut a large round out of each pastry sheet. Divide the vegetable mixture between the four pastry rounds. Fold pastry over and enclose. Seal by pressing edges with a fork. 4) Place pasties on a baking tray lined with non-stick baking paper. Bake in a preheated oven at 200 degrees Celsius for 20-30 minutes or until pastry is puffed up and golden. Serve with side salad or mixed vegetables.

Preparation Time: 15 Minutes

Cooking Time: About 30 minutes

Serves 4

Hoi Sin Beef Stir Fry

Ingredients	Method
500g Beef Strips **2 Carrots (cut thinly)** **1 Brown Onions (sliced into thin wedges)** **2 Sticks of Celery** **1/3 Cup of Hoi Sin Sauce (about 80ml)** **1/4 Cup of Hot Water**	1) In a lightly greased wok over medium heat, add beef and stir fry for 4-5 minutes or until browned. Transfer to a bowl and set aside. In a small jug, combine Hoi Sin sauce and water. 2) Add onions, celery and carrots to the wok. Stir fry for 2-3 minutes or until onions are lightly browned. 3) Return beef to wok. Add sauce and stir to combine. Cook for a further 2-3 minutes or until everything is heated through and sauce thickens slightly. 4) Serve with rice or noodles.

Preparation Time: 5 Minutes

Cooking Time: About 10 minutes

Serves 4

Nachos Bolognese

Ingredients	Method
500g Beef Mince **1 Brown Onion (chopped)** **2 Cloves of Garlic (crushed)** **1 Tablespoon of Olive Oil** **2 Tablespoons of Worcestershire Sauce** **2 Teaspoons of Dried Mixed Italian Herbs** **1 Jar of Tomato Pasta Sauce** **Grated Cheese** **Sour Cream** **Guacamole** **Corn Chips** **Mild Paprika**	1) Add oil to a medium saucepan over medium heat. Add onion and garlic. Stir for 2-3 minutes or until onions soften. Add mince and cook for 5-6 minutes or until browned. 2) Stir in Worcestershire sauce, herbs and pasta sauce. Bring to the boil, then reduce temperature to low. Cover and simmer for about 20 minutes or until sauce thickens. 3) Arrange corn chips on serving plates. Top with meat sauce, cheese, sour cream and guacamole. Sprinkle with paprika. Serve immediately.

Preparation Time: 5 Minutes

Cooking Time: About 30 minutes

Serves 4

Cheaters Tuna Risotto

Ingredients	Method
400g Can of Tuna (drained and flaked with a fork) 1 1/2 Cups of Arborio Rice (Risotto Rice) 1 Brown Onion (chopped) 50g Butter 1 Litre of Chicken or Vegetable Stock (4 Cups) 1 Cup of Frozen Peas Salt and Pepper Shaved Parmesan Cheese (to garnish)	1) Add butter to a medium saucepan over medium heat. Once melted, add onion and stir for 2-3 minutes or until onions soften. Add rice and stir for 1 minute or until all rice is covered in butter. 2) Add tuna and stock. Stir to combine. Bring to the boil, then reduce temperature to low. Cover and simmer for 15 minutes. 3) Add peas and stir thoroughly. Cook for another 2-3 minutes or until risotto is creamy and peas are tender. 4) Divide between plates and top with shaved parmesan cheese. Serve Immediately.

Preparation Time: 5 Minutes
Cooking Time: About 20 minutes
Serves 4

Teriyaki Chicken Burgers

Ingredients	Method
1 Large Chicken Breast Fillet **1/3 Cup of Soy Sauce** **1 Tablespoon Caster Sugar (Super Fine White Sugar)** **1 Tablespoon of Mirin Seasoning** **1 Clove of Garlic (crushed)** **2 Tablespoons of Vegetable Oil** **Bread Rolls** **Lettuce** **Tomato**	1) In a bowl, combine soy sauce, mirin, garlic and sugar. Stir until sugar is dissolved. 2) Cut chicken fillet in half. Slice the two pieces to make 4 thin slices. Add chicken to marinade mixture and ensure all pieces are completely coated. Cover with plastic wrap and chill for 30 minutes. 3) Add oil to a large fry pan over medium heat. Cook the chicken pieces for 3-4 minutes each side or until cooked through. 4) Cut bread rolls in half. Add lettuce and tomato and top with chicken. Serve.

Preparation Time: 5 Minutes + Chilling Time

Cooking Time: About 10 minutes

Serves 4

Chicken and Vegetable Pie

Ingredients	Method
1kg of Chicken Thigh Fillets (about 6 or 7 fillets, chopped into chunks)	1) In a large saucepan, melt butter over medium heat. Add leek and sautee for 2-3 minutes or until softened.
1 Leek (washed and sliced)	2) Add chicken and cook, stirring, for about 5 minutes or until chicken is browned.
30g Butter	
1 Cup of Mixed Frozen Vegetables (Peas, Carrot, Corn etc)	3) Add vegetables, broccoli, herbs and soup. Stir to combine. Cook for 1 minute. Transfer mixture to a round casserole dish.
1 Head of Broccoli (trimmed and broken into florets)	4) Brush egg around edge of casserole dish. Place pastry over dish and press down gently around edges. Brush pastry surface with remaining egg. Poke 3 vent holes on top of pie to allow steam to escape.
1 Can of Cream of Mushroom Soup	
2 Teaspoons of Dried Mixed Italian Herbs	
1 Sheet of Frozen Puff Pastry (thawed)	5) Bake in a preheated oven at 180 degrees Celsius for 40-45 minutes or until pastry is golden and puffed.
1 Egg (lightly beaten)	

Preparation Time: 15 Minutes

Cooking Time: About 50 minutes

Serves 4-6

Weekend Wonders

Fabulous dishes for when you have free time

When you have a bit of time on your hands, it's great to get into the kitchen and make something a little more complex than your basic "throw-together" meal.

Call me crazy, but I find it relaxing to spend a quiet weekend in the kitchen, pottering around, peeling vegetables and stirring things. It's sensual and good for the soul. Cooking isn't just about eating. It's a process of creation. It's an art form. Cooking can be relaxing, challenging, joyous, uplifting, inspirational and lots of fun.

I think one of the reasons I enjoy it so much is that cooking allows me to express myself. It's a creative outlet that I so desperately need. I'm definitely not a musician. My music teachers in high school all had nervous breakdowns when they realised I was fundamentally untalented. I even failed at playing the triangle! I'm not much of an artist either. While I enjoy painting and sculpture, I'd be embarrassed to show off any of my works. I'll stick to appreciating other people's art.

So my chopping board has become my palette. My pots and pans are my canvas. The ingredients are my paints and combined they become a symphony of colour, light, flavour and sensation.

This section of the book features some recipes that are a little more in-depth. Some are slightly more complicated than the average "One Pot Chef" recipe. Others are merely a little more fiddly. I've also thrown in some recipes that fit into neither category. They are simply delicious, filling dishes that are lots of fun to prepare. All are perfect for weekend cooking, or whenever you have a little more time to play with in the kitchen.

Slow Cooked Swedish Meatballs

Ingredients	Method
500g Beef Mince	1) Preheat oven to 180 degrees Celsius.
250g Pork Mince	2) Combine milk and breadcrumbs and set aside for 5 minutes to soak.
1 1/2 Cups of Fresh Breadcrumbs	
1 Cup of Milk	3) In a large mixing bowl, add beef, pork, eggs, allspice, nutmeg, dill, onion, salt and breadcrumb mixture. Using your hands, mix everything together until combined. Chill for 30 minutes.
1 Brown Onion (finely chopped)	
2 Eggs	
1/4 Teaspoon of Allspice	4) Shape spoonfuls of mixture into balls and place on a baking tray lined with non-stick baking paper. Bake in oven for 15 minutes or until lightly browned. Transfer to slow cooker.
1/4 Teaspoon of Nutmeg	
1 Teaspoon of Dill	
2 Teaspoons of Salt	5) Add stock to slow cooker and season with pepper. Cook for 2-3 hours on IIIGH or 4-6 hours on LOW.
1 Cup of Beef Stock	
1/2 Cup of Cream (Sour Cream / Heavy Cream / Pouring Cream etc)	6) Before serving, stir in cream and allow to cook for 15 minutes on HIGH.
Freshly Cracked Black Pepper	7) Serve with pasta, rice, noodles etc

Preparation Time: 15 Minutes + Chilling Time

Cooking Time: 2-3 hours (on HIGH) or 4-6 hours (on LOW)

Serves 8

Beef Bourguignon

Ingredients	Method
2kg Casserole / Gravy Beef (any cheap cut will do)	1) Trim and roughly chop beef. Add oil to a large flameproof casserole dish or heavy based saucepan. Brown meat in batches over a medium to high heat. Transfer meat to a large bowl and set aside.
1 Large Brown Onion (finely chopped)	
4 Rashers (slices) of Bacon (chopped)	
400g Button Mushrooms (halved)	2) Add butter to casserole dish and melt. Add onion, garlic, mushrooms and bacon. Stir and cook for 5 minutes, or until onions are lightly browned.
2 Cloves of Garlic (crushed - about 2 teaspoons)	
30g Butter	3) Stir in flour. Gradually stir in stock and red wine. Allow mixture to come to the boil, stirring, and allow it to thicken slightly. Return meat to dish.
Olive Oil	
1/4 Cup of Plain Flour	
1 1/4 Cups of Beef Stock	4) Add bay leaves, then stir everything together. Return to the boil, then reduce temperature to allow mixture to gently simmer. Put the lid on and cook for 2 hours, stirring every 30 minutes.
2 1/2 Cups of Dry Red Wine	
2 Bay Leaves	
	5) Remove bay leaves. Serve with rice, pasta, potatoes etc

Preparation Time: 15 Minutes

Cooking Time: 2 hours

Serves 8 -10

Chilli Con Carne

Ingredients	Method
500g Beef Mince (Ground Beef) **1 Large Brown Onion (chopped)** **1 Clove of Garlic (crushed)** **1 Long Red Chilli (chopped, seeds removed)** **700g Jar of Tomato Passata sauce (pureed tomatoes)** **2 x 400g Cans of Red Kidney Beans (drained and rinsed)** **1 Teaspoon of Ground Chilli Powder** **Olive Oil** **Salt and Pepper**	1) Lightly oil a medium saucepan and fry onions, garlic and chilli over a medium heat until onions softened and lightly browned. 2) Add mince. Break up meat with a wooden spoon while stirring. Once meat is browned, add chilli powder, beans and passata. Season with salt and pepper then stir to combine. 3) Bring to the boil, then reduce temperature and simmer for 20 minutes or until slightly thickened. 4) Serve with rice, pasta, vegetables or on it's own.

Preparation Time: 10 Minutes

Cooking Time: 20 minutes

Serves 4-6

Country Style Chicken

Ingredients	Method
4 Chicken Breast Fillets **1 Leek (sliced)** **2 Carrots (Sliced)** **2 Large Potatoes (Diced)** **1 Tablespoon of Flour** **2 Cups (500ml) Liquid Chicken Stock** **Salt and Pepper** **Olive Oil**	1) Lightly oil a large, flameproof casserole dish. Over a medium heat, brown the chicken breasts, then set them aside. 2) Add a little more oil to the dish, then fry leek, carrots and potato for 2-3 minutes. Stir in flour. Add stock and season with salt and pepper. Simmer for 5 minutes. 3) Return chicken to the dish. Place lid on, then place casserole in a preheated oven at 150 degrees Celsius for 45 minutes, or until chicken is fully cooked and vegetables are tender. Serve.

Preparation Time: 15 Minutes

Cooking Time: 45 minutes

Serves 4

Slow Cooked Beef Curry

Ingredients	Method
1kg of Beef (chopped into small pieces) 1/2 Cup of Plain Flour 1 Tablespoon of Curry Powder 1 Cup of Sultanas or Raisins 2 Onions (peeled and chopped) 2 Green Apples (cored and chopped, skin on) 2 Teaspoons of Crushed Garlic (2 Cloves) 1 1/2 Cups of Liquid Beef Stock Salt and Pepper (to season) White Rice (to serve)	1) Add beef to the slow cooker pot. Sprinkle flour and curry powder over the meat. Stir to combine. 2) Add garlic, onions, sultanas and apples. Pour in stock and season with salt and pepper. 3) Give curry a good stir to ensure everything is nicely mixed. Place lid on slow cooker and switch it on to the "LOW" setting for 4 - 6 hours. 4) Serve curry with rice.

Preparation Time: 10 Minutes

Cooking Time: 4-6 hours on LOW

Serves 4-6

Chicken and Spinach Lasagne

Ingredients	Method
1 Barbecued Chicken (meat stripped and shredded) **50g Baby Spinach** **Olive Oil** **1 Large Brown Onion (chopped)** **2 Cloves of Garlic (crushed)** **1 1/2 Tablespoons of Plain Flour** **1 1/2 Cups of Liquid Chicken Stock** **4 Fresh Lasagne Pasta Sheets** **Pepper** **250g Ricotta Cheese** **1 1/4 Cups of Freshly Grated Parmesan Cheese** **(plus extra for garnishing)**	1) In a large saucepan over medium heat, add a little oil, onions and garlic. Stir for 2-3 minutes or until onions soften. Add flour and stock, then stir for 3-4 minutes or until sauce starts to thicken. 2) Add 1 cup of parmesan cheese, chicken and spinach. Stir until chicken is heated through and spinach is wilted. Season with salt and pepper. 3) In a large, lightly greased baking dish, add one lasagne sheet. Top with 1/3 of the chicken mixture. Continue to layer the mixture and pasta sheets, finishing with a pasta sheet on top. 4) Combine ricotta and remaining parmesan cheese. Spread over the top of the lasagne. Top with a little more grated parmesan cheese. 5) Bake in a preheated oven at 180 degrees Celsius for about 35-40 minutes or until pasta is fully cooked and lasagne is golden on top. Serve with a side salad.

Preparation Time: 15 Minutes

Cooking Time: 50 minutes

Serves 4-6

Big Chicken Quiche

Ingredients	Method
1 1/2 Cups of Plain Flour **Pinch of Salt** **125g Butter (chopped)** **1 Egg Yolk** **3 Tablespoons of Water** **1 Cooked Barbecue / Roast Chicken (skin and bones removed, meat roughly chopped)** **5 Chopped Spring Onions** **8 Eggs** **600ml Cream** **1 Tablespoon of Dijon Mustard** **1 Cup (250ml) of Dry White Wine** **Salt and Pepper (to season)** **1 Cup of Grated Cheddar Cheese**	1) In a large mixing bowl, add flour, pinch of salt and butter. Rub butter into flour using your fingers until mixture looks like breadcrumbs. Add egg yolk and water and mix together until a dough forms. 2) Roll dough out and place in a large rectangular baking dish, ensuring pastry covers the bottom and sides. Trim edges as needed. 3) Add chicken on top of pastry. Sprinkle with onions. Season with salt and pepper. 4) In a large jug, combine eggs, cream, mustard and wine. Whisk until smooth. Pour over the baking dish. Top with cheese. 5) Bake in a preheated oven at 180 degrees Celsius for 40-45 minutes, or until egg mixture is set and cheese is melted and golden. Serve with a side salad or mixed vegetables.

Preparation Time: 20 Minutes

Cooking Time: 45 minutes

Serves 8

Cheesy Stuffed Crust Pizza

Ingredients	Method
2 1/2 Cups of Plain Flour (Sifted)	1) Add sugar, yeast and water to a cup. Stir to combine. Set aside for 5 minutes. Add flour, salt and pepper to a large mixing bowl.
7g Sachet of Dried Yeast	
200ml of Warm Water	
1 Teaspoon of Olive Oil	2) Make a well at the centre of the flour mixture and pour yeast mixture in the well. Use a round bladed knife to make cutting motions through dough mixture until it comes together. Use hands to finish mixing.
1 Teaspoon of White Sugar	
Salt and Pepper	
1 Cup of Mozzarella Cheese	3) Turn dough out onto a lightly floured surface. Knead for about 5 minutes or until elastic and smooth. Return to bowl. Cover with plastic wrap and set aside for 1 hour to rise.
1/4 Cup of Pasta Sauce (from a jar)	
1 Cup of Mozzarella Cheese	
1/2 Cup of Diced Bacon	4) Punch down dough, then knead for 2 minutes. Roll out dough to make a 25cm disc. Arrange ½ the mozzarella around the edge. Fold edge over to enclose.
2 Teaspoons of Mixed Dried Italian Herbs	
Freshly Grated Parmesan Cheese	5) Smooth sauce over pizza base. Top with bacon, herbs and remaining cheeses. Bake in a preheated oven at 180 degrees Celsius for 15 minutes or until cheese is melted and crust is golden. Serve.

Preparation Time: 1 hour
Cooking Time: 15 minutes
Serves 6

Mini Meatloaves

Ingredients	Method
500g Beef Mince	1) In a fry pan over medium heat, add a little olive oil, onion, garlic and ham. Cook stirring for 2-3 minutes or until onions are softened. Set aside to cool.
250g Pork Mince	
1 Brown Onion (finely chopped)	
2 Cloves of Crushed Garlic (about 2 Teaspoons)	2) In a large mixing bowl, add meats, eggs, parsley, barbecue sauce, breadcrumbs, salt, pepper and onion mixture. Using your hands, combine all ingredients.
200g Thinly Shaved Ham (shredded)	
Olive Oil	3) Roll meat mixture into 12 large meatballs. Place each meatball into the cups of a lightly greased muffin pan. Press meatballs down to flatten slightly and fill out the muffin cups.
2 Eggs	
1 Tablespoon of Dried Parsley Flakes (or use fresh)	
2 Tablespoons of Barbecue Sauce	4) Brush ketchup over each meatloaf. Bake in a preheated oven at 180 degrees Celsius for 25-30 minutes or until meatloaves are cooked all the way through.
2 Cups of Fresh Breadcrumbs (about 4 slices of bread)	
2 Tablespoons of Tomato Ketchup	5) Allow meatloaves to cool in the pan for 5-10 minutes before removing. Serve with vegetables or side salad.
Salt and Pepper	

Preparation Time: 10 minutes

Cooking Time: 30 minutes

Makes 12 Mini Meatloaves

Sweet and Sour Meatballs

Ingredients	Method
750g of Pork Mince (or any meat you like)	1) In a fry pan over medium heat, add a little olive oil and onion. Cook stirring for 2-3 minutes or until onions are softened. Set aside to cool.
1 Cup of Fresh Breadcrumbs	
1 Small Onion (finely chopped)	2) In a large mixing bowl, add meat, egg and onion Using your hands, combine all ingredients. Roll meat mixture into meatballs. Lightly brown meatballs, in batches, in a fry pan over medium heat and place into a large casserole dish.
1 Egg (lightly beaten)	
400g Can of Pineapple Pieces in Juice	
2 Tablespoons of Corn Flour (Corn Starch)	
1 Tablespoon of Brown Sugar	3) In a large jug, combine juice from pineapples, sugar, vinegar, soy sauce, ketchup, garlic and water. Stir in corn flour until dissolved.
2 Tablespoons of White Vinegar	
1 Tablespoon of Soy Sauce	
1 Tablespoon of Tomato Ketchup	4) Add pineapple pieces and capsicum to meatballs. Pour over sauce mixture. Gently stir to combine.
1 Teaspoon of Minced Garlic (about 1 clove)	
1 Red Capsicum (aka Bell Pepper, sliced)	5) Bake in a preheated oven at 200 degrees Celsius for 30 minutes or until meatballs are fully cooked and sauce has thickened. Serve with rice or noodles.
1 Cup of Water	

Preparation Time: 20 minutes

Cooking Time: 40 minutes

Serves 4-6

Thick Tomato Soup

Ingredients	Method
1kg of Tomatoes (chopped) 500g of Potatoes (peeled and chopped) 1 Brown Onion (chopped) 2 Cloves of Garlic (chopped) 3 Cups of Vegetable Stock (750ml) 2 Tablespoons of Tomato Paste Olive Oil Pepper Handful of Fresh Basil Leaves	1) In a large saucepan, add 2 tablespoons of olive oil. Over a medium heat, fry onion and garlic for 2-3 minutes or until onions soften. Add tomato paste and stir through. 2) Add tomatoes, potatoes and stock. Season with pepper. Stir everything then bring to the boil. 3) Reduce temperature and simmer soup, covered, for 20-25 minutes or until potatoes are tender. 4) Allow soup to cool for 5-10 minutes. Stir through basil leaves. Blend soup in batches until smooth. Serve with crusty bread.

Preparation Time: 20 minutes
Cooking Time: 25 minutes
Serves 4-6

Measurement Conversions

METRIC CUP & SPOON SIZES

Cup	Metric
¼ Cup	60ml
1/3 Cup	80ml
½ Cup	125ml
1 Cup	250ml
Spoon	Metric
¼ Teaspoon	1.25ml
½ Teaspoon	2.5ml
1 Teaspoon	5ml
2 Teaspoons	10ml
1 Tablespoon	20ml

LIQUIDS

Metric	Cup	Imperial
60ml	¼ Cup	2 fl. oz
100ml	1/3 Cup	2 ¾ fl. oz
125ml	½ Cup	4 fl. oz
180ml	¾ Cup	6 fl. oz
250ml	1 Cup	8 ¾ fl. oz
500ml	2 Cups	17 fl. oz
1 Litre	4 Cups	35 fl. oz

MASS (WEIGHT)

Metric	Imperial
30g	1 oz.
125g	4 oz. (¼ lb)
250g	8 oz. (½ lb)
500g	16 oz. (1 lb)
1kg	32 oz. (2 lb)

OVEN TEMPERATURES

Celsius	Fahrenheit	Gas Mark
120	250	1
150	300	2
160	325	3
180	350	4
190	375	5
200	400	6
230	450	7

ABOUT CUPS:

To make things easier, when you see a recipe in this book asking for "1 Cup" of an ingredient, use any measuring container that holds exactly 250ml of water. That is the correct size of the measurement, regardless of what ingredient is being measured.

PLEASE NOTE:

This is a basic conversion chart and does not contain all possible conversions. If you require further information, there are several online resources available. Do a Google search for "Australian Measurement Conversion Chart" and you will find more complete conversion charts.

Index

Sausages in Brown Onion Gravy	24
Slow Cooked Beef Curry	40
Slow Cooked Swedish Meatballs	36
Spaghetti Puttanesca	10
Stuffed Mushrooms	26
Sweet and Sour Meatballs	45
Teriyaki Chicken Burgers	32
Thick Tomato Soup	46
Toad in the Hole	21
Tomato Pesto Pasta Salad	14
Turkey Burgers	18
Tuna Macaroni Bake	11
Vegetable Pasties	28

Notes

CPSIA information can be obtained
at www.ICGtesting.com
Printed in the USA
LVHW072133080719
623510LV00016B/581/P

‖‖‖‖‖‖‖‖‖‖‖‖‖‖‖‖‖‖‖
* 9 7 8 1 1 0 5 8 8 9 2 6 4 *